THIS is
ME

Marty Tilley

EXPLORA BOOKS

700 – 838 West Hastings St. Vancouver, BC V6C 0A6

www.explorabooks.com

Phone: (604) 330 6795

ISBN: 978-1-997587-40-8 (Paperback)
978-1-83430-075-7 (Hardback)
978-1-83430-116-7 (eBook)

This is ME

MARTY TILLEY

Table of Contents

Part Four

About the Author

Marty Tilley, with a degree in psychology and post-graduate work in communications, has spent almost twenty years adapting to a disease that is steeped in a cloak of mystery and darkness. Today, she continues her research on a farm in Adams, Tennessee.

Dedication

Dedicated to the ones I hold close in my heart: Ed, my husband, my soulmate; Lance, Catherine, and McLean, my awesome children; Riley "bug," Lincoln "beebs", Monroe "boat," and Jackson 'Jack Jack', my precious grandchildren.

Acknowledgement

I wish to thank the ones who have helped me along the way, unaware of their strong impact on my life. I wish to thank the scientists, spending countless, and often, thankless hours in the laboratory, trying to find a cure for these vague, ever-elusive, neurodegenerative diseases afflicting millions.

A personal thanks I wish to extend to Dr. Robbins for saving my life, and a joyous thank you to Dr. Lieberman for continuing to do so.

To my husband, I say thanks. You provide love, strength, and a safe haven when I need it most.

To my children and grandchildren who keep life worth living, I say thank you.

To my earthly father, thanks for being with me from the very beginning of my life, and never giving up on me, as well as a big thanks to my sister and forever brother who will always have my back.

I wish to thank my mother, for sacrificing absolutely everything so that I might live. I will never forget as long as I have a beat left in my fragile heart.

And I wish to thank my heavenly father above who has kept me alive to share this incredible story and, hopefully, touch hearts, with hope, healing, and love.

Marty.

Prologue

Given a life sentence in May 2002 paralyzed me to the core. Feelings of sadness, yes, and even awe, swirled inside me as I sat while the specialist loaded my arms with books and pamphlets. To get here, we must return to the beginning.

"Is it only with the heart that one can see rightly; what is essential is invisible to the eye."

– The Little Prince

Part One

1

Weighing less than three pounds, fitting in a shoe box, with the face of a tiny, shriveled rat, this is me. A screaming preemie, mad, and quite vocal about it, I enter the world one Thursday evening so long, long ago. A lifetime ago.

Earlier, my mother calmly sits in the automobile, while dad tosses the suitcase into the backseat. This suitcase is different. No soft blankets nor hand-smocked gowns from her mother, are tucked inside. The little one will not make it. The two of them understand and drive to the hospital in silence.

The toxins are raging throughout my mother's body now and she can no longer wait. Delivery of the fetus is the only cure for eclampsia.

During the beginning of her pregnancy, she had waited. Against her doctor's advice, she had waited. As her family and close friends urged her to proceed with the delivery, she still waited and for this reason, in that small, rural hospital, to the amazement of the doctor, the staff, and my parents, I survive. I was their noisy, scrawny miracle. I had survived. Three years later, my mother did not.

Remaining in the hospital for the next two months, I thrive. Parents of premature infants today, are given literature detailing possible outcomes for their little one-learning disorder, blindness, deafness. One half will have abnormalities in the brain. Support groups are available today. But in 1955, they were not. My parents took me home and prayed.

2

At the age of three and motherless, Dad and I move into his parent's home. My aunt, Dad's sister, recently divorced, had moved in as well, with her baby boy. The two of us immediately bonded, like true brother and sister, growing up in this loving, safe environment for many, many years.

In that tiny home, with a gigantic backyard, in proportion to our tiny legs, we played together, climbed trees together, and our imagination soared. Why, we even ran away together, to join the circus!

We, however, did not get very far. Fifty feet. Then, we knocked on our neighbor's door, who had the farm with the farm animals, always waving to us whenever grandmother drove by her house. Announcing to her our bold plans of running away and in desperate need of a drink of water, "please ma'am," she obliged and immediately, phoned our grandmother.

The disappointment seen in the eyes of someone you love and hold so dear in your heart, truly does hurt more than any quick pop on your bottom. And we never spoke of running away again.

Years pass, and Dad offers me a tiny glimpse into his inner thoughts, which was a very rare occurrence. Right after the move and burial of my mother, he allowed himself only one week to mourn. At age twenty-four, now widowed, and with a stubborn child to raise, he knew he must return to some type of normalcy. So, he returned to work.

He had, after all, promised my mother, as she lay dying, he would take care of me. He has never let her down.

I remember very little of the farmhouse we called home, while my mother was alive. The home had no bathroom. None did, in the '50s, in rural America. I, thankfully, still wore diapers.

Happiness is what I do feel with the memories I recall – tiny kittens scratching my arms, while I stuff them into my baby stroller; little ducklings, dyed purple, circling my feet, as I squat for a photo, in my Easter best.

Quite poignantly, and somewhat foretelling, I recall us leaving a church service. Giggling, I sail through the air, leaping from the church's highest step, into the arms of a teenage girl. I can still see her face. Not my mother's – the girl's.

Coming from strong genes, I continue to flourish, like my Dad, still working each and every day at 86. My maternal great-grandfather, born in the late 1800s, began a logging and sawmill business with a team of mules; with no one questioning his sanity whatsoever years later, as he spat tobacco juice on the floorboard of his brand-spanking new Cadillac, and my paternal great- grandmother, cooking over a wood-stove, birthing babies, and working in the fields, alongside her husband.

Living to be almost 100, she was baptized, in her late 80s, in a bathtub. St. Peter had a huge smile on his face when "Ma Nettie" appeared at the pearly gates. Dipping for as long as I can even recall, I believe the first question she probably asked upon arrival was quite simple: "Where do we get our snuff?"

And to this very day, I still use an old "snuff" can to cut out my angel biscuits, in remembrance of Ma.

So many ancestors, with unique strength and resilience, and I find that I am, thankfully, becoming one of them. This journey has opened my eyes to the plasticity within each of us, if we allow the growth to take root.

I understand we all have our "crosses" we must bear. Some people decide to bypass, ignore certain "crosses" because the pain is just too difficult. And I cannot judge, nor will I, the personal struggles or injustices an individual may encounter in this fragile world we live in.

I do know my own mother, after delivering a full-term baby boy, a mere eighteen months after my miraculous birth, turned her back as they brought him, lifeless, a few hours later.

One year passes and she joins him.

3

During the 60s, peace, love, and harmony were dreams people hoped for, longed for, and I was just beginning to enter the first grade. In the mid- 60s, turning 13, finally, a teenager, wearing bell-bottoms, having long, straight hair, that I straightened each morning with my stepmother's iron, I hoped to change the world; just as the Coke commercials advertised daily on our television.

Imagine a group of girls, in a circle, singing kumbaya, and you capture the essence of the only weeklong camp my dad ever allowed me to attend away from home. Conservation Camp, at Kentucky Lake, offered a week with nature, and before the end of the week arrived, each cabin was required to participate in the camp's annual talent show.

Many, many years later, watching the movie "Dirty Dancing," with my teenage daughter, I was transported immediately to those cabins, and I could see us each morning, preparing for the activities of the day, whether they be swimming, archery, hiking, or canoeing. And then, after the last snack from the nearby canteen, frantically searching for some type of talent, hidden in our little bungalow.

Of course, a few things were obviously different. We had no parents in our camp, only cool counselors with cool nicknames, and probably, not much older than we were at the time.

Stumbling across a guitar player in our cabin, who happened to bring her guitar along, we voted unanimously, to sing. And before we even had a chance to miss our family and friends, the week was near an end and the talent show was upon us.

Seated on the ground in a circle that warm Thursday evening, we sang a song quite popular in the 60s, titled "Where have all the flowers gone?" before the entire camp. Every verse we knew of this soul-searching song, a song of hope, written by Pete Seeger, we sang.

At this tender age, we were completely unaware of the significance of our choice, being simply naive, while at this exact moment in time, in large cities, bomb shelters were being constructed. We did, however, know one thing. We won first place.

Roaring into our school one morning, in the early 70s, a student sauntered down the hall, with a mane of hair as thick as a lion's and falling onto his shoulders; an authentic hippie, or at least in my eyes, just as I began my junior year.

All he needed was the sign, with the large peace symbol emblazoned across it, stapled onto a thin piece of wood recently purchased at the local hardware store. Immediately, I felt fresh air enter these stale hallways, with boorish decorations, ancient artifacts, and apathetic students.

Walking in, wearing a sleeveless, white, muscle t-shirt and frayed-bottom jeans, he stayed mere moments and was sent home. No one, absolutely no one, wears muscle tees in this school.

Smitten, I longed to meet him, and hear of his travels, his ideas, his future dreams. And I did. Spending countless hours together during study hall at school, we would discuss practically everything.

On our dates, he located amateur plays in small-town basement libraries. I developed my love for the theater through these productions, filled-to-capacity with fellow theater enthusiasts.

Never dreaming our last date would be the final time I would see him; I assumed his silence stemmed from either an injustice he had just become aware of in our "world" or his sister once again, arguing with him that "Dark Shadows" was a better tv series than "Mash." I was wrong on both counts.

The day he left; a teacher also left. She left her husband, her family, her career, and this humdrum town, for him.

Then I decided to grow up. I tossed away my rose-colored glasses, for good.

Always analyzing people, I majored in psychology when I began college, longing to study their behavior, as a scientist studies a specific organism. With hippie days long behind me, I concentrated on pursuing a career in a position that I hoped would bring me joy. In the 70s, the primary emphasis on attending college, meant obtaining your ideal job, first and foremost, while, hopefully, providing you with a respectable salary.

My fascination for the field of neuroscience has developed recently, due to my illness, and another very important reason. At the age of six, I flew.

Able to crack a 7 mm. skull in a single leap, I soar through the air, flop head first onto the floor, and I do not move. I should have known better, but my brother had climbed those attic steps and I followed wherever he led.

The ambulance made record speed, hauling my little body to Nashville, after the doctor emphasized to "spare no horsepower!" And after almost twenty hours unconscious, with a neuro-surgeon on standby, I awakened. The doctors inform my Dad there is no brain damage. Another miracle.

Six years come and go, and a letter appears in the mail from the hospital I had been in and of course, I immediately panic. No good news could come after all these years, and indeed, I felt that major, devastating news lay inside that envelope. To my surprise, as Dad explains, these doctors are simply requesting a follow-up x-ray, now that I am twelve. I am not sure why they chose six years, but I go and allow this hospital a glimpse of my skull once more. Hopefully, they will not find any horrible residual from my traumatic injury.

They return, after the x-ray, with astonishing news. They could not find the site of the original break, at all.

Years later, when I am at my specialist's clinic in Charleston, S.C. he clarifies for me the role of MCS1* and how it often attacks the weakest part of one's body. So, sadly, it seems my right-sided hemiparesis and degeneration are resulting from my one attempt to fly.

---

1. * MCS, multiple chemical sensitivity, also known as idiopathic environmental intolerances, IEI. It is a complex chronic condition which manifests as a result of low- level exposures to certain everyday chemicals.

4

In a small town, in a small school, in a small class, my education commenced, simple, predictable, with one exception. My parents had also walked these hallowed halls. The significance of this could not be appreciated until I became much older.

My memories are few, until the third grade. After lunch, on 22 November, we return to our assigned seats for our next lesson to begin and our teacher enters, tears in her eyes, and a Kleenex in her hand, to inform us the President of the United States has been shot and is dead.

We were too young to fully understand the seriousness of what had just transpired in our beloved America. However, the rowdy eight-year-old boys in our class, remained solemn and stoic for the rest of the afternoon. By the fifth grade, the real world knocked a little closer to our little haven, having my small, brown, suede purse, fringed, with a long shoulder strap and a hint of embroidery, stolen from my dilapidated, archaic, locker.

Our lockers didn't even lock. Why? Who could possibly want anything from our hick town?

A new girl had enrolled in the fourth grade, and being new, I assume she had no idea how poor we, collectively, were in this school system. Having no consistent intercom system, the principal's voice reverberated throughout the halls, for all to hear and fear. Mimeographed tests were the only source of duplication for the teacher or staff, and blue ink stained everything, hands, shirts, and notebooks nearby. The milk we drank in the cafeteria each day at lunch always tasted somewhat spoiled, since it was lukewarm and disgusting.

Hard working, blue-collared workers comprised most of the town's population, with the exception of one doctor and one banker.

Stealing my purse, according to the teacher, would allow her a chance to eat. I had never even heard of "hunger," except for the television commercials, urging people to donate to the starving children in third world countries.

By no means were we ever, ever rich, but we always had food on the table. Dad planted a garden each year and my stepmother cooked the harvest. It was that simple, or I had thought it was that simple.

Asking for my beautiful purse to be returned, I suggest the young girl keep whatever money I had in my wallet, if any. The grown-ups recommend the girl apologize to me, and I, being very shy, whisper, "No, thank you." I did not wish to relive this embarrassing situation each and every time our paths would cross in the hallway, and they would, being such a small school, with less than 200 students. So, the invisible face remains invisible, and I pray her family never goes hungry again.

5

Within a few months after college graduation, I jumped at the first job offered to me. Divorced, with a four-year-old son, the need for a job was vital and I had to grab the first opportunity, which turned out to be as a social worker for the state of Kentucky. Never could I have dreamed the trajectory this position would launch my career path towards, but I do know I learned many life lessons, while working for the state; patience, compassion, empathy, and strength, especially whenever testifying before a judge. Unforgettable, my very first job, and shortly after beginning, it became unbearable.

Soon, I say "I do" once again to marriage and life, as a stay-at-home mom, when later, my family blossoms into two more adorable little ones, about twenty-one months apart. As a family of five, we learn farm life, with John Deere gator mishaps, painful paintball battles, and grueling motorbike races, ending in scraped knees and bruised egos. I hate to even mention the day I burned down the detached garage, complete with stored ammunition for the hunting rifles and boxes of old, leftover fireworks from the previous 4th of July events.

With gunfire blasting, fireworks shooting towards the sky and the one-eyed, Chesapeake Bay rescue dog howling, the sirens begin. An ambulance, a fire truck, and two police cars are soon arriving in record time, considering we live in the country. Neighbors appear from nowhere to offer assistance, curious and fearful, I'm sure, of the endless sound of gunfire. As the vinyl siding on the house begins to melt, I rush into the house and retrieve one item, my daughter's wedding dress.

Often people are asked, what if anything, would they grab should a fire ever occur in the home, and I can honestly say now, a wedding dress, especially when the wedding is less than a month away.

While my two youngest ones were still toddlers, I longed to enter the workforce again. Knowing this second marriage was doomed, I had to realistically consider my children's future. My second husband had difficulty keeping steady employment, whether it be on his dad's farm, working for his uncle's company, or beginning his own start-up construction company. He would have been an ideal candidate for the "gentleman" era, we read about in the novels of Henry James or Leo Tolstoy, who identified the upper-class "gentleman" as well-to-do, sporting a devil may care attitude, and spending their days in gaming and foxhunting.

I searched vigilantly, in the private sector, since previously working in a government position. With the red-tape, never, ever ending, I told myself it was time to enter the private world.

A newly opened psychiatric facility, "Rivendell," needed a marketing /public relations representative. Being an avid Tolkien fan, I knew this job was the one for me, and they agreed. Once again, I was part of the millions employed.

In Tolkien's books, a place of safety, respite, and healing, was aptly named, "Rivendell." How fitting to name their hospital after this fictitious place, as they open their doors to help the mentally ill. I never imagined someday I would wish for my own "Rivendell" to heal my broken body.

Seven years later, and a new physical-rehabilitation facility opens its doors. With my current boss leaving her position to work for this new hospital, I soon follow. Now, my market base would include – medical professionals, physicians, case managers, social workers, as well as, the opportunity to evaluate and educate potential patients for our rehab facility. And with the joy I received from these encounters, I planned on working with this company for a very long time. I could not see this huge demon hovering over me.

Nine years, entering patients' rooms, evaluating, meeting their families, the physicians and case managers, day after day, all is well. For over 1,800 individual moments, the days were routine. Until, they weren't.

Part Two

6

Heading to the first-floor emergency room, after excusing myself from the patient's room, a medical team begins administering life-saving treatment. Hours later, returning home, slightly groggy still from the Benadryl-epinephrine cocktail, I realize a very important page in my life has just been turned and I haven't the faintest idea why.

Looking back, the red flags, the warning signs, the proverbial "hindsight is 20/20" ringing in my ears, all of it became clearer, much later. But during this unique period of my life, I viewed each allergic episode as an isolated incident, never dreaming how interconnected they truly were becoming. Even the allergy specialists treating me, felt the episodes were coincidental, desultory.

Like a complex riddle, clues were everywhere if I could just solve the equation. I also knew that I would have to be the one to crack this case of "me." As a reporter in high school, for our small-town newspaper, I knew what to do. Instead of focusing on high school events, I would investigate me.

Every good reporter begins with the issue at hand, the background data, the current situation, and any future predictions, and finally, proceeds with the findings: the truth. I had myself to provide the issues, the current predicament, but I lacked any background data, for this entity wrestling within me. My resolve is strong, however. Time is of the essence, too, knowing deep down in my soul, I am dying.

Trip after trip to medical doctors, allergy specialists, and each seems puzzled by my onslaught of symptoms, which some thought were of significance and others deemed totally irrelevant. I knew one thing, as my allergic reactions increased, my right-sided strength decreased.

Trying to remain hopeful, daring myself to enter the world, ever-mindful of my life slipping away, I limp into a bookstore. Long before smartphones, I had very little recourse other than the old-fashioned way – books.

People stare as I limp in. Like at the circus, I am the main attraction, the death-defying beardless lady. My eyes hollow, skin wrinkling, toxins rampaging throughout my body, I look frightful I am sure. Today, I will not allow this phantom in my body to consume me. I will search until I give it a name, an identity. This was my chance. Could the accuser we learned about in Sunday School class be taunting me, asking, "Hey, just who do you think you are?" It took me a long time to come to terms with the answer.

Stumbling upon a book titled "A to Z in Allergies," I purchase the very thick, heavy paperback, and immediately return home.

Glancing through the table of contents and finding a chapter called "Chemical Sensitivities and Allergies," I just knew. So, I began to read. And read. My life literally leaps off the page. I smile. Feeling ill, I still smile. The diagnosis I had been diligently seeking for over a year, is staring back at me.

Quickly turning to the resource index, I read specific names of environmental specialists, complete with their address and telephone number. I discover distance will be an issue for me, since these specialists have clinics in Arizona, California, and New York, not to even mention the European countries. Since I cannot risk a trip by plane, I know I will need to drive, and then I see his name.

One specialist is in Florida. This state is very familiar to me. Growing up, Dad would take us every summer to the beaches in Florida, for fun and relaxation. How funny he was during our vacations as he would wake us up early, reminding us, "You can sleep when you get home." Looking back, I see the wisdom of his words – "Grab the moment! Seize the day!"

– and I chuckle. Dad exposed us to this philosophy long before the popular movie "Good Will Hunting" was ever written. Carpe diem, Daddy.

Making the call to Robbins Environmental Center, in Boca Raton, instills excitement in me, as I speak with his nurse, seemingly for hours, and yet, only minutes, of my countless doctor visits, ER visits, and basically, all the unexplainable symptoms I have endured. A week and a phone consultation later, I have an appointment. How fitting that my doctor visit will be in May, the month of my birth. I had one more appointment left with my allergist, which I will wholeheartedly admit, I dreaded, having spent countless terrifying hours in this clinic.

The allergist had suggested to me, finally, a "patch test" for possible chemical sensitivities, to be administered on this date. Although my mind was already sixteen hours away, thinking of Boca and the chance for healing, I went.

A "patch test" involves placing a sterile, gauze patch, containing certain identifiable chemical compounds, on a person's clean, lotion-free back. For the next twenty-four hours, the instructions are clear – no baths, no scratching and return the following day.

Heading home, with the patch firmly attached between my shoulder blades, I begin to experience discomfort. But undeterred, I plan to endure this annoying patch.

A few hours later, the discomfort escalates to the feeling one has when standing too close to a fire, thereby causing your synapses to signal the brain that danger is fast approaching. Immediately, I phone the allergist- on-call.

He was unsure exactly how to advise me, in this precarious situation. He cautioned that removal of the patch would compromise the test results. However, if I did choose to return tomorrow, an allergist would be available to examine my back. Ending our conversation, he simply reminded me again, the results might be inconclusive.

Hanging up the phone, I rip the patch from my back, swallow mega-doses of prednisone, and shower, counting the minutes for my histaminic episode to subside. I wish the allergist, after our conversation, had charted his clinical notes in greater detail.

After receiving my massive file from the allergy clinic, hoping to deliver it personally to Dr. Robbins, I am dumbfounded when I read the final note placed in my chart. It simply read: "She removed the patch before the allotted time and did not return the following day."

Sad. That one sentence cost me over three-quarters of a million dollars.

*When the time had come to renew our employee benefits, about the mid-90s, new options were offered and I checked the box for long-term disability insurance. Traveling one to two hundred miles each day for my job, I felt my chances of a car accident growing exponentially, and the extra expense of the policy would be deducted from each paycheck, which always worked better for my brain, out of sight and out of mind. The policy was very specific about the definition of the disability, "The employee is disabled when he/she is unable to perform the position currently held in the company." After sixty days, the policy would begin to pay 60% of the current salary. I knew this would be a financial cushion for my family should anything drastic happen to me. This company I had been contributing to each paycheck, year after year, chose that allergist's one note, in that small, final paragraph, to stamp my claim – "Denied." After submitting a five-inch file, complete with comprehensive blood work, tests, and an attached letter from my specialist in Boca, their answer was still a resounding "No." Thousands of dollars later in lawyer fees and their answer becomes a defiant "NO!" My claim is closed, filed away in some long, forgotten basement. I guess Edward Bulwer-Lytton was correct – "The pen is mightier than the sword." The same file, the same tests, the same blood work, and the attached letter from the specialist, were simultaneously mailed to the Social Security Administration Office, in Washington, D.C., with my completed application for disability. Uncle Sam, with his pointing finger, solemnly responds, "Yes." And I crumble to my knees in thankfulness.

7

Resting on the beach, with my daughter and then-husband, provided a much-needed respite for us before Monday's appointment, with the new specialist.

Sick, but excited, I drove us to the clinic, located in Boca Raton, one of the wealthiest communities in Florida. The evidence surrounds us, as we each marvel at the coral and cream buildings, the manicured grounds with palm trees standing large and proud, and of course, the automobiles; the Rolls Royce's, the Bentleys, the Mercedes G Wagons, and the list goes on and on. I was just happy that my old BMW made it and we had finally arrived.

Luckily, our hotel was just a few miles away, in Deerfield Beach, allowing my daughter and her dad to have the choice of returning and enjoying the beach, while I stayed for the appointment.

Banyan trees welcome us, with their large, gnarled roots, growing upside down. I must capture their magnificence and their strangeness, so I quickly snap a photo before we enter the clinic. These trees are gnarled and twisted, like me.

Upon entering, I see them. With hollow, deep-sunken eyes, wrinkling, opaque skin, a mere shell of their former self, they sit. Albeit depressing, it uplifts my spirits, finding patients like myself. These people know me without saying a word.

Walking towards Dr. Robbins' office, I catch glimpses of Old Testament scriptures, framed, decorating the hallway, and I find comfort in this. Dr. Robbins, with very wise, knowing eyes, extends his hand and welcomes me to the clinic. We smile and I know everything is going to be just fine. He has a guitar painted on his tie, and soon, I discover he loves Nashville, country music, and even writes songs.

After the examination and medical history gathered, he explains that he truly believes he can help stop my progression of this dreadful illness coursing through my body, which he labels "MCS." However, his next few words devastate me. "There is no cure."

Now, I completely understand the look I saw in my fellow patient's eyes upon entering the clinic; one of utter sadness and despair. May God help us all.

Environmental toxins, he continues, are "overloading" my internal workings, liken to a barrel overflowing with water. He plans to reduce the overload, which is destroying my immune system, with his detoxification program – exercise, sauna, deep tissue massage, with nutritional supplements and Vitamin C IV therapy, twice a week.

I am beginning to see his vision. A tornado is brewing deep inside me; highs and lows are converging together, ready to annihilate everything in its path, leaving nothing but destruction behind. And Dr. Robbins plans to rebuild.

Mere minutes from the clinic and a block from the beach, I noticed one morning, a sad, dilapidated motel, with a "for sale" sign in the courtyard. Much of the motel consisted of freestanding cottages, and it was at this moment, something inside me clicked. This would be an ideal location for MCS sufferers, with access to the ocean nearby, ready to offer fresh breezes and relaxation.

Sharing this vision with my then-husband proved futile. He had recently inherited his portion of the family farm and had been contemplating a career change. I knew these patients would benefit greatly from a motel opening just for their specific health issues. However, he explained it was too much of a financial risk, buying this old, run-down motel. I still think it was a good idea.

Beginning, the detoxification program was an experience like no other. Taking physical-education classes throughout high school was our daily ritual of exercise, thanks to President John F. Kennedy, and his launching of the Presidential Medal of Fitness. Our coach dreamed of one of us achieving such a medal.

Each year, he would choose a specific day, for the designated activities and the competition. With his trusty stop-watch and whistle, he methodically recorded the results from each activity; each race, each jump. Quite grueling and intense, I must say I lacked winning this medal by one score, being too high, in the 50-yard dash. Dr. Robbins' program left me in the dust.

Perhaps, due to the severity of my illness, I had little endurance. Perhaps, experiencing the dry sauna for the first time in my life, aptly termed "the dungeon" by the patients, drained me of every ounce of strength I could muster. Perhaps, seeing dark flecks of toxins emerging from my skin, intermingling with sweat oozing from my molecular system, frightened me a little. Regardless, I survived.

In two weeks, I realize I will be heading home with boxes of vitamins and supplements, and a concoction to drink, consisting of magnesium, calcium, and buffered C powder when I encounter a toxin, thereby reducing the possibility of losing consciousness. The irony of me ingesting magnesium isn't lost on me, I promise. Pregnant women in the hospital today, are given magnesium IV treatment when suffering eclampsia. How I would love to tell my mother the mineral they administered to her that fateful day, is still coursing through my veins.

I remain hopeful, when I return, my then-husband will believe these results and will never ever consider an option one patient shared with me, while we were each waiting for the doctor. For her unexplainable, unimaginable symptoms her husband could fathom no longer, he committed her to a psychiatric ward. These heartbreaking stories were a daily occurrence; the sharing, the praying, the tears, and even laughter, yes, even laughter occurred as we waited our turn with the wise man.

One singular, common thread among MCS sufferers, really surprised me. It involved perspiration. Dr. Robbins explained that every single one of his patients had difficulty sweating. Disconcerted, I began to remember the times I would almost faint, while playing sports in high school. Red- faced and clammy, I would stop and allow my body to cool down. Our bodies have their own unique, cooling-down system; over 2.6 million sweat glands and none of mine work.

Entering the doctor's office after a few days of detoxification, he hands me a copy of my blood panel and a three-act murder mystery began to unfold in my head; "Arsenic, Mercury, and Lead." However, in this situation, the victim isn't dead, yet. Intrigued, I begin to scan the list of compounds; massive information obtained from a few vials of blood.

Having a high level of lead came as no surprise, having been educated forever through ads and commercials about the horrors of lead paint used eons ago, in our schools, our government buildings, and basically, everywhere.

Mercury being very elevated, was somewhat surprising. Still, with my mouth full of decades-old mercury fillings, the probability of the metal releasing into my bloodstream, I could understand.

The third level, which was high, caught me completely off guard. Arsenic? How does one even obtain arsenic? I had only heard of it in Agatha Christie novels, and never dreamed it could really be lurking in our blood, eager to strike.

When undertaking this research, many years after receiving these results, I chance upon a postgraduate's paper completed in Australia, detailing arsenic and its devastation. "Arsenic toxicity is a global problem, affecting millions. Contamination is caused by arsenic from natural geological sources leaching in waters." (Ratnaike) He states, "Arsenic is one of the most toxic metals, and is used to manufacture, 'paints, fungicides, insecticides, pesticides, herbicides, wood preservatives, and an additive in some animal feed.'"

In concluding, he stresses, "The neurological system is the major target for the toxic effects of arsenic, mercury, and lead." And, I have all three. This is me, "Arsenic, Mercury, and Lead." Last act, and the curtain goes down.

Reading my mineral lab results proved just as eye-opening. This was the true inner part of me; blood, guts, and all. Manganese, it would appear, is high, which means my body will suffer with symptoms of fatigue, low blood pressure, deterioration of memory and tremor. Being positive for every single one of these symptoms, I felt I was sitting before a psychic, waving her arms frantically over her crystal ball; findings spewing forth, rapid and cruel from the sides of her mouth. The truth, sharp and real, hit hard. My molybdenum level is low, which is especially troublesome for me since its main function is to assist the body in detoxification. My selenium is low, therefore, causing my body to be more susceptible to inflammation when exposed to chemicals. I understand more fully my increasing sensitivities to almost everything now. My zinc level is high, which results in symptoms of fatigue, difficulty writing, and problems with fine motor skills. Now, I am truly shocked.

Recalling one of the last conversations I had with my boss before leaving the job I loved, she had explained to me their concern for me months before I even told them the bizarre happenings

They were seeing it; seeing it through my handwriting. Completing the evaluation forms for potential patients to be admitted to our rehab facility required extensive writing. They watched as mine declined.

Finally, they were having difficulty even deciphering the words I penned. They had said nothing to me. Absolutely nothing. I am so humbled by it all.

Now, with my blood providing him the information, from metals to IgG subclasses and T cells, Dr. Robbins developed an individualized treatment plan just for me; and after return visits to Boca and the too-many-to- remember phone consultations with tweaking throughout for optimal results, he maintains my health status over sixteen hours away.

It was heartbreaking to hear from his nurse, many years later, that he would be closing his practice due to health issues. This specialist, who saved my life, could help himself no longer. A physician appears invincible to his patient, able to defy any germ that tries to invade their body, and yet, deep down, we know the truth. These superheroes we admire and trust, are only human, after all.

Throughout these visits, my internal medicine physician, Dr. Peach, located within an hour from me, continued to treat me whenever he could. From the early 2000s, a seemingly quiet, unassuming antibiotic, then another one, and another, would react dangerously in my system; yet, he persevered, trying to identify one antibiotic that my body would accept without the horrific anaphylactic result. For over twenty years, he has provided me with optimal care, and when he could do nothing, he listened. And at my annual examination, he will order the necessary lab panels and blood work to assess the health of my internal organs.

MCS strikes mysteriously, deep inside a person, when they are completely unaware, and will harm the vital organs, such as the liver and spleen. MCS attacked my liver, in '09, requiring hospitalization. Thankfully, a recheck four weeks later, showed no lingering damage. Another miracle.

I read of a successful college football coach, in Massachusetts, around the year 2004, who wasn't as fortunate. In a wheelchair, he continued to coach from the sidelines, until finally, he could not. About two years after his diagnosis of MCS, he died.

MCS does not cower in the corner, but stands tall, upright, like the bully in the schoolyard, daring the sufferer to fight. It wins every time.

After returning home from Boca, I often dreamt of an astronaut-type suit, lightweight, with compartments for oxygen to filter throughout, and, of course pockets, to carry all the medical necessities. This would allow people, as myself, the freedom to explore. Instead of the moon, we would be exploring Earth.

Being much more practical than a bubble suit/apparatus, this suit would be comfortable enough to wear while driving. Seeing the portable, oxygen machines, which were becoming more readily available, the oxygen issue would be minor. The issue, undoubtedly, would be the cost. The first prototype would be astronomical.

I researched more capable masks to wear, respirator-type ones, commercial-grade, industrial-strength ones, and fire-fighters' masks; finally, I stumbled upon a very interesting one, made in France. This mask reminded me of the knitted ones we wore as children, when the weather turned cold outside, with small openings for our eyes to peer through, and an ever-so-tiny opening for our mouth, allowing gulps of hot cocoa to partially enter our mouth cavity. With the eye openings and a Darth Vader- appearing mouth, the ad proclaimed, quite convincingly, the MCS sufferer would be protected from most toxins and would feel safer when leaving their home.

I must admit, I loved the concept. My fear, however, was in misconceptions, when driving into town wearing a dark, fully covered face mask.

Not long after my dream of an astronaut suit, I had another idea, which would bring attention to the plight of MCS and other neuro-degenerative diseases; the screen.

"House, M.D." had recently become a major television hit series. Every week, "House" would diagnose a difficult case, unlock the key to the patient's mysterious, life-threatening illness and they would improve. I composed a script of a degenerative illness, i.e. MCS, and mailed it to Mr. Laurie in Los Angeles, for his perusal. A few weeks later, I received a letter from his assistant, informing me that he was in England, and yet, she wanted to personally forward the script. I was elated. I was stunned. Bad news came soon afterwards, however. The writers informed me they did not accept outside scripts for this series.

Explanations to a layman, as to what exactly comprises a multiple chemical sensitive patient, are daunting at best. The sufferers have their own unique symptoms of varying degrees, from mild to life-threatening, and most are self-reported, as are most of the neuro-degenerative symptoms at the onset. For this reason, the general field of medicine views us, with a broad microscope, unable, or possibly, unwilling, to delineate these reported symptoms from psychosomatic ones.

Our vital signs, upon entering the emergency room or a physician's office, mimic the appearance of anxiety-related problems; increase in blood-pressure, pulse skyrocketing, and rapid breathing. After a toxic exposure, our body reacts in a fight-or flight-mode, which we learn about in high school biology class. Gathering its army together, the body protects the inner workings of the central nervous system and intends to succeed.

I cannot help but admire the sheer power that our body can wield against itself, to protect itself.

Once the battle begins internally, our pulse will rise, along with our blood pressure, and our breathing will become shallow and fast. I am imagining Clint Eastwood directing a film, depicting the internal violence and turmoil deep within and aptly naming it, "The Good, the Bad, and the Ugly, Too."

Yes, this is me, a preemie, born in a hospital with no NICU equipment for sustenance; a cracked-skull child with partial hearing loss, a Heimlich Maneuver survivor caused by a fatty prime rib, and a countless Epi-Pen winner, each and every time administered. I do feel qualified to testify before the court of skepticism and inform the jury that indeed, miracles are happening.

Now determined more than ever, I focus on this demon with all the intensity I can muster, beginning with the naysayers, to finishing the journey, with truth and hope; hope to sustain us, to motivate us, to help us keep the faith, and remove the cloak of darkness, stepping into the light once again. I have been snatched from the jaws of death too many times to not complete this mission.

8

Isolation, loneliness, quiet sadness can be deafening and can occur in a roomful of people. After almost twenty-five years of marriage, the inevitable became apparent and divorce was imminent. For over a year, I had been alone, night after night. When this illness strikes, it leaves no one upright. No longer needing to pretend, divorce becomes the final answer. The beautiful silver lining for me, is the peace in my heart, knowing my children, now basically grown, will have no other woman tucking them into bed at night. Strike two on marriage, I must concede. However, when it comes to my death-defying moments, I'm losing count.

With my divorce finalizing, my heart began to remember my one love while I was in college. We dreamed of marriage, kids, building a home on the farm, and all the future joys young people dream when so in love. Sometimes, unfortunately, the future takes a sharp turn and we are left stranded in the street, holding nothing but our crushed love.

Unaware of his marital situation, I simply mail a card wishing him a Happy Valentine's Day, since this date was fast approaching. What would his reaction be? Surprise? Hatred? Placing the card in the mail, after finding an address and praying it was him, I sent it, signing my name and my cell phone number. As in chess, the next move would be his.

After four days, he phones. When I hear his voice, the love flows through my heart, awakening again, from almost thirty years of being forgotten. To commemorate this special first date, I wait until Valentine's Day. We have been together since that moment and married four years after that first date.

When I first discovered I had MCS, I read of the utter isolation this diagnosis brings; another level, a lower level of darkness. I have looked down that deep, dark hole of despair, and I chose to not enter. It can become so easy to release our dreams once held and allow these demons to envelop us and overtake our lives. However, we can begin to stand and choose to not accept this isolation as the final word. I was so impressed by a gentleman's spirit online, in an MCS chat room so many, many years ago. Although seriously ill, he had one goal, to arise every day and "hammer one nail into one board" for the new home he was building. With that spirit of determination, I have no doubt he succeeded.

With each of us, no one can say what is just over the mountaintop we are trying so hard to climb every day, but we must continue the hike. Another human being, a potential soulmate, or a wandering soul, lost and needing help to find their way, waits on top.

As George Eliot wrote so eloquently, 'What greater thing is there for human souls, than to feel that they are joined for life to strengthen each other in all labor, to rest on each other in all pain and to be one with each other in silent, unspeakable memories at the moment of the last parting.'

9

Like David facing Goliath, shouting, "This day I will defeat you," my illness holds no more fear, now that I know my nemesis by name. With my specialist in Boca no longer practicing, the time has come to search once again. This time is different, because I know what I seek and I know why. My entire life depends on it.

A search on the internet, and one name shines bright and piques my interest, as Dr. Robbins had done, in '02. The specialist practices in "The Holy City," and I need another miracle.

Hope, mixed with relief, is soon restored again in my heart, once I finish my call to Dr. Lieberman's clinic, in Charleston. The Holy City, thusly named, for the abundance of church steeples outlining the sky, had been a city my husband and I longed to visit, but never had. Now, necessity beckoned me to this town, filled with history and culinary delights. We reserved lodging in their historic district, an inn that once was an old, cotton warehouse. Joy fills my heart as we journey towards our destination, and I thank God above. I will meet this well-known specialist, who has been treating patients very similar to me, for over thirty-six years. And soon I will become one of them.

Thank goodness, this illness has no unknown demons lurking in the back alleyways, all previously identified and labeled by Dr. Robbins. He has kept me alive. Now, life is pushing me in another direction, eastward to South Carolina, the state of my favorite vacation spot, where we would take our family, while I was working and healthy – Hilton Head. The beach will not welcome me this trip, however, for I have just a few days to see the doctor and no time to head to this relaxing island, in the shape of a foot. Upon meeting Dr. Lieberman, I am seriously awestruck.

The Academy Award winning movie, "A Beautiful Mind," pops in my head as I shake hands with him; not for the schizophrenic portion of the movie, but for his brilliant mind you become aware of immediately, once he begins to speak. Without further delay, his nurse practitioner enters, explaining she will take an extensive evaluation/history, if you will, of "me." She stresses the importance of leaving nothing out, medical, physical, anything that I might think trivial, but wish to express, from my birth to the present day. Having never been asked this question quite this way before, I begin and I cannot stop. These memories come rushing forth like a stream, continuous, with snags, debris, yet, still moving. I share it all and then, sit, exhausted.

After several hours, we break for lunch, and I return to meet with Dr. Lieberman. Before him, sits my file with a polaroid of me snapped earlier and stapled in the front left corner. My life, all the bloody gore, spilled out earlier to the nurse practitioner, is neatly typed and placed inside the folder.

Quietly, he reads my story, and then speaks, "On behalf of man, I apologize." Tears fill my eyes.

Silently, I thank God above; this specialist I am seeing was absent that fateful day in medical school, long ago, when the professor taught the proper protocol for taking medical histories of patients. The professor explained, "You will learn sooner or later, that the more numerous a patient's complaints, the less significance of any of them." (Chicago Tribune, Jan. 1993)

10

A drop of hope under my tongue and a tiny capsule compounded from ingredients found in the jungles of Vietnam, are two additions Dr. Lieberman prescribes for me after seeing promising results from his other MCS patients. Eager to try something new after being on a maintenance protocol for years, I am glad to become a guinea pig, and hopefully, reap some of the benefits of these two promising compounds.

Envisioning a tiny jet, loaded with the necessary weaponry to shut down the synapses wreaking havoc in my brain, I swallow the pill. From 9 a.m. to 2 a.m., they complete their mission. Then, a miracle happens. In the morning, when I awaken, my brain's synapses will awaken "with a vengeance," explains Dr. Lieberman. I can see my brain lit, an aurora borealis inside my head, and am absolutely spellbound by the entire process, not only for me, but the sufferers of multiple sclerosis and Parkinson's Disease, who are benefitting from this, as well.

Realizing the compound originated from Vietnam, conjures up another picture in my brain, of an eight mm. film I watched while visiting my aunt and uncle in Mississippi, as a young child. Being only nine, I stared at the images moving across the screen, of women and children in a muddy river, washing clothes, splashing in the water, enjoying the day.

As little children, I remember well, the lantern-shaped contraption we had, with slots for the strips of colored-film to poke through and shine images of Mickey Mouse to our delight. We projected the images on the largest screen we could find; our grandmother's dryer.

I see, finally, up close, my uncle's main purpose in Vietnam. Flying this enormous plane, he hovers over a jet, mid-air, to re-fuel, allowing continuation of the battle in the air. I am impressed and saddened.

Often, I picture my aunt and uncle sipping espresso together at one of the small cafés in Paris, unencumbered by life's tragedies and what would ensue. My uncle often spoke of the Douglas beauty, known throughout the land, and I know he saw it in my aunt and her sisters, with one being my mother, of course. I finally got to see it, the day my baby girl was born.

These two sisters' correspondence, oceans apart, brought much comfort to me through these dark moments. Reading in the letters, my aunt's growing concern for her sis – "Did you get a new haircut? Have you been to the doctor lately?" – imply a hidden meaning; a sister's worry that something is going horribly wrong. My mother ignores the questions completely, and writes an epitaph, detailing the two of us shopping at the local five-and-dime store – and, like the King Tut treasure, she spots the "loveliest white comb." My aunt writes of Paris and my mother writes of a lovely comb, a comb that she did not even buy.

Yes, I am becoming a human guinea pig and I do not mind. I fell in love with guinea pigs, while watching the children's show "Wonder Pets" with my baby granddaughter. To this very day, I am not sure who loved the show more, her or me. The guinea pig, not the guinea, of course. Hopefully, the guinea hen and I will never cross paths again.

Playing outdoors while Dad was in the yard, we, so little and so fearless, never see the baby chicks, nor do we attempt to touch one, being much too busy running and jumping. The guinea spies us, flaps her wings, spreads her talons, and begins chasing us.

Running, I leap onto the front porch before my brother, who stumbles. She is atop him, pecking his eyes. I still see this image, over sixty years later. Dad, still outside, hears the screaming, the loud squawking, and frantically grabs a rock, and hurls it at the angry hen with incredible force. The rock completely misses the guinea hen, hitting the fencepost nearby, ricocheting, and landing dead center between the hen's eyes. She topples over instantly, and Dad is our superhero; my brother has both his eyes, and such goes another day for us.

Part Three

11

Upon launching my research, some may wonder why it has taken almost twenty years after my diagnosis to begin. The answer is quite simple: acceptance.

Strange thing about the final stages of grief. As you accept the finding, the results, and the verdict, you stagnate. It is not even a conscious decision. You throw in the towel. Well done, you have won, friendly foe. Go forth and tease me no longer. Go seek your next victim.

I had reached the end of my rope, with the cold reality of my illness staring back at me in the mirror, and I wished to enjoy what quality of life I still had. Fighting so hard to be understood, I was tired, so tired, trying to explain the unexplainable.

Reading those books, the ones the specialist had placed in my arms, and even ordering more, the literature had reiterated his very words. Avoid the toxins and the triggers, at all costs. Your life depends on it.

Having an older BMW allowed me to drive a little, with the new car smell long gone, and no perfume whatsoever to complicate matters. This car has such significance for me, having slept in it many nights.

Travel was familiar, having been such an integral part of my life, for over seventeen years, as a marketing rep for hospitals. One thing I hoped to keep enjoying, was the exhilaration of the open road. If I respect my boundaries, be very cautious, I can, on occasion, take a drive.

Many nights I'd gather my purse, toss on my old Burberry trench to disguise my PJ's, and pretend I was whole again. Sometimes, I would stop at a Starbucks, and walk in briefly, for a cup of coffee. Then, it would be my coffee and me, driving, observing the sights and sounds of the world for a little while. I wish I had purchased stock in that new coffee shop so many years ago.

Beginning this search, I hope to find definitive, objective and measurable data to validate this illness the medical world approaches with skepticism and scorn. Being a psychology major, I would also like to respectfully suggest one more stage to be listed at the end of Dr. Elizabeth Krueger Ross' iconic "Five Stages of Grief"; after "acceptance," add "complacency."

Complacency delves further into our inner core, as it plays on the inner psyche day after day, and our tiny flame deep inside, flickers, and goes out. It will extinguish after the hundredth time we enter the physician's office and hear our symptoms are too numerous; the patterns of the said symptoms are too difficult to measure, and to simply, return home and stay…forever.

On an existential level, I never, ever, questioned why now, why me. I knew. Bad things do happen to good people. And I have been both good and bad. My words cast no blame. Most people in our incredible world will experience very few problems with toxins and chemicals, and most assuredly, not to the degree I have experienced.

After a spiritual reawakening, I began to feel emotionally strong enough to handle whatever results I might uncover. I am finding myself eager to begin, an unearthing, if you will, like an archeologist striving to find that one ancient fossil which will connect a long-lost city to today's civilization. With this adventure, I must wear multiple hats, and the number one hat will be that of a human being trying to exist in this world.

My re-awakening came after listening to my favorite podcast, by Joel Osteen. His words always manage to uplift and inspire. After hearing his, "From Patient to Physician," I began to thaw. He states, "When you have been through the pain of a loss, a divorce, an illness, and been through the valley, it gives you a unique perspective that others cannot know…

You have been through the loss, the treatments, and are uniquely qualified to help others going through the same problems." The tiny flame buried deep inside me began to fill me with warmth, passion, and determination to fight with every fiber of my being, like the true warrior I am becoming. Growing up in church and having been baptized since the age of 14, I missed attending the services, after the development of this debilitating disease.

A couple of years after my diagnosis and much experimentation, I devised a simple way to hear the preacher and the congregational singing on most Sundays. By placing a simple, inexpensive, baby monitor, plugged in at the pulpit, and having the second one with me outside in my car, I could hear the sermons once again.

Keeping a songbook with me, I sang along, quite loudly, to my audience of one, which is a good thing. I am a terrible singer. The only time I have ever sung in public, was at a funeral with my stepmother, my best friend, and a gentleman from our church, singing a few hymns for a poor soul, who lost his life playing Russian Roulette.

12

I am ready, so ready, to press on and grasp any relatable, documented studies to identify "me," and soon I discover one published in the "Journal of Nursing Education and Practice." Titled "Unmet medical care needs in persons with multiple chemical sensitivity," (2015) I discover my assumptions are indeed correct. According to this article, the issue of true verification and validity for MCS as a disease, remains even today. Patients, suffering with this degeneration, are shying away from any medical care until the dreaded emergency occurs. These patients, being so sick, have little information to draw from while the physician questions every symptom they convey. If the physician looks close enough, MCS will be visible and will be horrifying to behold.

Limping into that specialist's office, in '02, Dr. Robbins saw. I would have been an ideal "extra" for the series "The Walking Dead." And truth be told, I felt like it.

Once beginning this research, I found an interesting article from Italy, written by a group of industrial experts, who had compiled a framework of the "MCS syndrome" and presented it to the Italian government for approval, in a bill titled, "Bill N 1922." They hoped to enlighten their medical community, with the varied and different stages of progression, thereby helping the physicians, as they attempt to understand this illness and offer help for their patients. The statements concur with the definitions and specific terminology I have collected over the past year and a half, regarding definitions, symptoms, and the severity of the MCS illness; from mild to life threatening.

In the first stage, zero tolerance, the individual is normally able to adapt to the environment that surrounds him, unless the limits for certain hazardous substances are exceeded.

The second stage, sensitization, is a result of chronic exposure to low doses and/or after an individual's acute exposure. The patient may complain of the following problems: dermatitis, respiratory irritation, itching, fatigue, muscle and joint pain, headaches, nausea, tachycardia, blood pressure problems, cognitive issues, asthma, insufficient peripheral circulation and gastrointestinal diseases.

The third stage, inflammation, means a chronic inflammation in different tissues, organs and systems. Various disorders for development are detectable through examination such as: dermatitis, vasculitis, immune, endocrine, and metabolic diseases, allergies, arthritis, colitis, rhinitis, asthma, muscle fatigue, fainting, cognitive delays, and poor peripheral circulation. The persistence and aggravation of this stage depends on the exposures, their avoidance and if a patient undergoes any therapy.

The last stage, deterioration, means chronic inflammation producing damage to tissues and organs, the central nervous system, kidneys, lungs, liver, immune system, circulatory system, vascular and lupus. Heart failure, cancer, autoimmunity and neurodegenerative syndromes are the most common disorders in this stage.

And, I look closely, and must admit, it comes as no surprise, I am in the last stage. C'est la vie.

The need for identifiable, clarification of the illness, of its very existence, appears vital, as I continue further and learn of Denmark's concerns. Their physicians are experiencing a marked increase in patients with self-reported symptoms of MCS (The Environmental Illness Resource, March 2013). Within one year, almost 70% of them reported having been consulted by at least one MCS patient. Over half of the doctors reported the complaints as chronic, stating they had felt "ill prepared to meet their patient's healthcare needs." Thus, they referred them to other medical specialties. And 90% of the physicians told the patient the same words: "Avoid the exposures."

Pressing onward, I must continue digging, sifting, trying to piece the puzzle together, and find validation for those of us who suffer. We are real and multiplying in numbers. And then, I found some things.

13

"Reliable disease biomarkers" began one article published in "Environmental Health." (2015) The authors explain, "The identification and measurement of reliable biomarkers is a crucial step for identifying and characterizing diseases." They focused their research on finding specific biomarkers which could identify electromagnetic sensitive patients and MCS patients, who more often than not, suffer with both issues.

These researchers measured the brain-blood flow in the cerebral hemispheres of MCS patients by using the echodoppler, to measure the brain's pulsatility, and an ultrasound to measure the blood flow in the different areas of the brain. Their hypothesis was straightforward – the MCS patient would show neuro-inflammation and blood-brain barrier disruption in the testing.

Our blood-brain barrier protects us from the nasty toxins and chemicals entering our brain, allowing the necessary, vital cells, to enter. I can just imagine a watchdog, always diligent, protective of its master; the brain. Sometimes, however, the dog gets tired, possibly injured, thus allowing the brain to be more vulnerable to an attack. I can see MCS sufferers experiencing this very thing. I must admit, I am excited to be reading actual tangible testing that could possibly link our illness to scientific results and, at the same time, I am devastated to realize the precious protective barrier to our brain has weakened and is now vulnerable.

The team, also, measured an inflammation-associated high-sensitivity C reactive protein and levels of D3 in the patient's blood. Vitamin D deficiency is linked with "abnormal development and functioning of the central nervous system." Histamine levels in the blood were measured, as well, and were quite remarkable. Brain injuries, neuro-degeneration, and inflammatory responses to toxins, can result in massive high levels of histamine release in our bodies. "Neuronal histamine" has been shown to be involved in the "sleep cycle, motor activity, synaptic plasticity in the brain, and memory...all types of neurologic, altered symptoms in the sufferers," stated the researchers.

As they predicted, the vitamin D3 levels were very low in the group of MCS sufferers studied; the levels being an actual consequence of the dreadful illness and not a cause of inflammation. Therefore, the team recommended the medical professionals address the vitamin D level with their patients. Then, comes the exciting part.

By utilizing the cerebral tomosphygmography, they found that the patients with MCS, in comparison to the control group's results, had "decreased cerebral pulsatility and abolished pulsatility in one or both temporal lobes." The researchers even saw evidence of this brain alteration resembling that found in Alzheimer's patients and other neurodegenerative diseases. They infer the chemicals' main target, in MCS sufferers, is the brain. And these researchers utilized readily available biochemical tests, and ultrasonic cerebral tomosphygmography, which would be accessible to the medical world.

In conclusion, the group explains, "Medical professionals should avoid the frequent erroneous interpretation that these patients are psychosomatic...and are genuine pathological entities." I am so happy to be acknowledged as an entity, while I weep for each of us who suffer, and our impending outcome.

When reading about an opening to my brain, I must give pause. An article, in "Encyclopedia of Occupational Health and Safety," claimed a loss of the blood-brain barrier's capabilities to restrict toxins can be caused by many and varied attacks; one being trauma to the brain. And I am once again reminded of my need to soar indoors.

Upon dissecting this medical terminology, the words may seem intimidating, almost disconcerting, at first glance, but for an MCS patient, they provide the key to critical, verifiable data. By implementing simple medical tests that can be performed using blood samples from the patient, I am now learning of significant scientific data being gathered. So, my mental door opens wider.

In 2004, a team of scientists studied over 200 MCS cases with 160 subjects in their control group, and found significant differences between these groups in pertinent genetic markers (a genetic marker, in our bodies, is a DNA sequence with a known location). The genetic polymorphisms were identified as: CYPD206, NAT, NATZ, PON, and PON2. I will admit these sound like possible names for the next droid in an upcoming Star Wars film, but the findings are huge – clear, precise, identifiable markers that only we MCS sufferers possess. (Journal of Epidemiology, 2004) I am beginning to feel less and less like the elusive BigFoot or the Lochness Monster.

The "Journal of Neurological Science" (2009) published measurable data, which, I must note, has serious and very frightening conclusions for MCS sufferers. Their research focused solely on brain dysfunction. They were concerned the patients' SPECT results might change after a chemical exposure (SPECT is the type of medical-imaging equipment used). In comparing the results with the control group, the findings were astounding, and utterly devastating.

MCS sufferers showed major, decreased blood flow, known as Hypoperfusion, in their brain – the right parietal lobes, the temporal and fronto-lobes. Hypoperfusion appeared in the right and left hippocampus, right parahippocampus, right amygdala, right thalamus, right and left Rolandic and right temporal cortex regions. Just as one might imagine, this is basically every part of the brain, and the evidence is irrefutable.

MCS sufferers have decreased blood flow throughout the vital regions of their brain. Our brain is under full-blown attack by this "demon" of an illness. While I still can, I tip my hat to MCS and say, "Touché."

Another similar study involved subjects from many different countries – the United States, Canada, Australia, Russia, China, Middle East, and Africa. The researchers identified in the patients' blood, several biomarkers that were specific and remarkable in the MCS population.

The protein SlOOB was markedly increased, which is associated with brain damage. And two others, melatonin6-OHMS and creatinine, which they measured in a 24-hour urine test, showed major declines, thus causing the patients' immune system to grow weaker, increasing their risk for developing severe chronic diseases.

This definitive data was gathered by usual, routine blood tests and medical imaging, using an MRI and a carotid echodoppler. With the echodoppler, the group found cerebral hypoperfusion in the patients, just as the earlier study I cited, had shown. And, they too, concluded in their final statement, "The abnormality is similar to that of Alzheimer's patients."

With watering eyes and a grateful heart, I read further, one paper after another, outlining scientific, verifiable data for these degenerative diseases that are causing millions upon millions, pain and suffering, ending in death. Yes, things have progressed in the scientific world.

Countries, such as Australia, Great Britain, Japan and Denmark are diligently searching for answers to every symptom, every seemingly quirky pain, a patient may be experiencing. It would appear some of the scientists and physicians are no longer compartmentalizing medical diagnoses as mere black and white; realizing a muddled mixture of both entities, developing new shades of gray, in the identification and classification of diseases. With a piercing plea, one researcher in Japan, stresses the urgent need for an updated definition of "toxicity," since the one, currently in the medical books, is virtually archaic, in this modern world we live in.

As my favorite author once said, "The real voyage of discovery consists not in seeking new landscapes, but in having new eyes."

14

Identifying a conference meeting in Brussels, May 2015, I eagerly downloaded the article with bated breath, praying for significant findings and it did not disappoint.

Experts from European countries and North America, gathered at the Belgian Royal Academy of Medicine, in Brussels, for the 5th Paris Appeal Congress dedicated to "hypersensitivities to electromagnetic fields and multiple chemicals." In locating the group's website, I observe illustrations, accounting for the electromagnetic and multiple chemical sensitivities co- occurring in so many of the MCS patients. This illustration is fascinating and incredibly terrifying. This drawing depicts my brain.

The brain, in a prior research study I mentioned, does, indeed, have its own barrier for protection. However, in our case, as MCS sufferers, we have acquired a "second pathway" through this barrier. The route, developed from toxins crossing the intestinal barrier, entering our blood stream, and finally, crossing over the BBB (Blood-brain barrier), is literally chiseling out a second path.

With this access to our brain cells, certain neurons may be destroyed, leading to neuro-degenerative diseases. When other cells overreact and try to compensate for this loss of neurons, a brain tumor can potentially develop. The seriousness and sheer devastation of it all overwhelms me.

Another key piece I find is from Dr. Pall, a professor of biochemistry, at Washington State University. He has developed the NO/ONOO-Cycle, which many have termed a "revolutionary" discovery. It is appropriately named after the nitric oxide that he feels is a toxin and treats it as such in his theory.

In his diagram, I see arrows connecting to more arrows, stimulating the variable of the next arrow, etc., etc., in our brain, "each having a mission to perform, the connections continue to work together, stimulating one another." (Pall). He further explains, "the challenge comes, in MCS, to lower this pattern of elevations."

To me, I liken it to my first few knitting lessons, when viewing his diagram of the Cycle. My loops are loose and when, inadvertently I add another unnecessary stitch, the next row will have a loose, dangling loop, which will be in danger of unraveling. My blood-brain barrier's permeability has loosened, just as my first knitted loops did. The unraveling of a scarf doesn't quite compare to the unraveling of one's brain.

It would appear Dr. Pall began his research into chronic fatigue syndrome and similar illnesses, after he personally was diagnosed with chronic fatigue. In an article recently written by Dellwo, "The Pall Protocol for Fibromyalgia and Chronic Fatigue Syndrome" (August 2018), he explains Dr. Pall has developed a treatment protocol, to help patients whose "build- up of naturally occurring nitric oxide" is starting this vicious cycle, leading to long-term illness. Many studies are supporting his theory of these "dysfunctional pathways" and many of the sick are proclaiming the protocol is helping them. Reviewing the list of recommended supplements, I am, once again, transported to Boca, seeing the first protocol supplements individualized for me.

"Nitric oxide is all over the body and plays important roles such as influencing oxygen transport to your tissues and transmitting nerve impulses," Dellwood, a supporter of Pall's, surmised. Thus, with high levels of NO, the central nervous system will receive tissue damage. He lists Dr. Pall's possible "stressors" – viral infection, bacterial infection, physical trauma, carbon monoxide exposure, organophosphorus pesticide exposure, toxoplasmosis infection, volatile organic solvent exposure, autoimmune diseases.

The most fascinating piece in this article, and something I will never, ever forget, was the final remarks of Dr. Pall's research. Dr. Pall explains the vicious cycle is "happening at the cellular level," which is why one tissue can be in pain while the ones around it are not. Therefore, this gives a precise, clinical explanation as to why the symptoms can vary so vastly from one patient to another one. Kudos, Dr. Pall.

This truly has been the "thorn in my side" as I try to legitimately be recognized by the medical community, who view the MCS sufferer as voicing pointless psycho-babble, spouting symptom after symptom. And with little chemistry education, I still understand and even more importantly, respect "Biomedical Pharmacology" article in 2010, as they emphasize the sheer delicacy of our cell structure. They recommend, "to map these pathways in various systems for different ligands, cell types, and exposure conditions, to aid in predicting safe exposure levels and identifying susceptible human populations." And my damaged brain considers the true magnificence of these cells, composing our very existence, and the utter devastation that can be thrown toward them in surprising ways from the environment.

Part Four

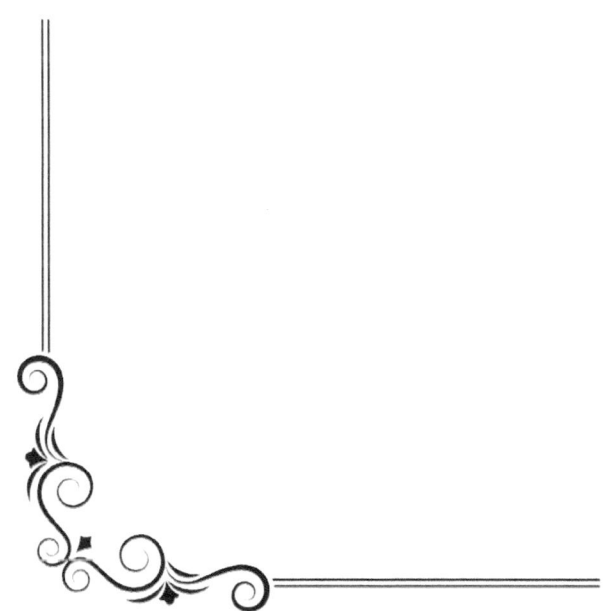

15

Dr. Lieberman has recently prescribed sulfa glutathione, a mighty warrior of supplements. Discussed within the medical world in 1889, it has only been in the past 30 years that scientists have begun to understand how vital it is to our human bodies.

This master antioxidant is in every cell of our body, every single one of them. It protects our DNA, maintains our inner proteins to keep their proper form, and wakes up our enzymes, allowing them to carry out their functions. Like the superhero it is, the sulfa portion of glutathione attaches to the toxins and frees the glutathione of all the toxic molecules. "With this supplement, we keep our immune system on the ball and fully armed," states Dr. J. Gataun, in his book Glutathione. Your Body's Most Powerful Protector. I can just see our friend, a super-plumber all by himself, cleaning and restoring equilibrium once again, as he bends over each molecule, with his tattooed, clown face, strategically placed on his backside, smiling right back at you.

Impressive, sulfa-glutathione can cross the blood-brain barrier, to detoxify and protect the brain, which is crucial for MCS sufferers, whose barrier's permeation has loosened, allowing toxins to enter and evoke havoc in the brain.

He adds to my regiment, the supplement PQQ, for mitochondrial support. The mitochondria, a part of our cells, supplies power and energy to our vital organs. In fact, the mitochondria are responsible for more than 90% of the energy needed by our body to sustain life. Since the mitochondria cells decline as we age, this supplement promotes new mitochondria for youthful cellular energy production.

And to specifically target my own right-sided hemiparesis, he explains, "This PQQ supplement will positively impact the damaged nerves and help them recover."

Nerve growth factor s.o. Sublingual drops are also added to my repertoire, for a one-two punch – the ngf, to promote growth and maintenance of nerve cells, and the s.o. will help the scarring deep within my brain, from my flying escapade.

Reading the patent for this Streptolysin O, one finds amazing results from the case histories submitted to the patent office. Dosage of the sublingual drops ranged from one to six drops a day, having two units of streptolysin per drop. One patient, female, reported that, after three weeks of treatment, the severe acne "scarring her chin" was softening. She reported "improved ability to move her mouth without the tightness caused by the scarring." After thirty days of treatment, another female patient reported that the burn scars on her hands "had faded and were entirely clear." The examples continue, each one impressive and encouraging, and so uplifting, to hear these people's lives being changed from these tiny drops. Now, I pray these tiny droplets will conquer my internal brain scar tissue from my fall, at the ripe age of six.

I read of the company, RESOLYS BIO, INC., formed in 2016 and a "spinout" company, of Beech Tree Labs, Inc. Their definition of the company is direct, "a clinical-stage biotechnology company focusing on therapeutic agents for chronic disorders" with concerns for traumatic brain injury, and chronic tissue disorders, such as joint hypermobility syndromes, Lupus, Rheumatoid Arthritis, and Fibromyalgia. This group is using streptolysin O for chronic traumatic brain injury, to "potentially reverse many of the cognition, motor, memory, mood, and personality deficits." The s.o. functions as "a biological signal molecule to help restore normal cell communication." And at Harvard Medical School, a study of concussed mice, after the administration of s.o. drops for several days, showed these mice as having the same level of memories, as the non- concussed mice.

This is awe-inspiring, and now, I can see Dr. Lieberman's mission. Dr. Robbins' gave my body an upstart. Now, Dr. Lieberman continues by recharging my central nervous system and reigniting my scar tissue's cells. And, I am anxious, apprehensive, and over-the-moon with anticipation to see what might occur after a month, two months, three, of taking this s.o. treatment.

Along with the sublingual drops and my drink concoction, I now have an arsenal of options to assist me and protect me from losing consciousness or having a cardiac episode.

16

I must admit, one of the most surprising finds after 18 months of research, beyond my identification of objective and measurable validation, involves the MCS brain and possible parallel studies involving other neurodegenerative diseases. I learned this illness attacks my body's inner connection to internal and external factors, with countless, incongruent variables challenging my system daily. And, I know that scientists are offering hope for our disease through their diligent research. Now, I know even more.

Imagining our blood-brain barrier, as it loosens, offering this second pathway, as researchers are claiming, I cannot help but wonder. In Bio Med Research (July 2014), the researchers, in regards to administration of drugs for brain diseases, clarify that the "BBB acts as a physical barrier and imposes various obstacles. It inhibits delivery of therapeutic agents to the central nervous system and imposes obstruction for delivery of a large number of drugs, including antibiotics, antineoplastic agents, and neuropeptides, to pass through the capillaries of the brain."

And they conclude, "there is a need to generate new nanosized carrier vehicles that could easily pass through systemic microvascular beds found in blood capillaries and endothelial cells for safe delivery of pharmaceuticals." And I have an epiphany.

With our pathways degenerating, loosening, as it were, the medical professionals might be able to determine other avenues and entryways, from our extra "routes" we are developing deep inside our brain, to help them attack these diseases that are practically unreachable. With over 55 million people diagnosed with MCS, surely a possibility exists somehow, somewhere.

I understand BioMed's concerns when they warn about the loosening of the patient's brain barrier, via medical manipulation that may alter the "homeostasis of the brain and result in seizures and compromised brain functions." (July 2014) As an MCS sufferer, I must remind them, our barrier is being compromised each and every single moment we exist.

17

Having dreamt of a Rivendell for my own, personal healing these past seventeen years, I found one, well, about as close as anyone possibly could, in beautiful Switzerland, nestled in the Alps. The Zurich House opened in 2013, by an MCS sufferer, Christian Shifferle, who had become ill when very young, after exposure to toxic fumes in his parents' furniture factory. He explained, "All my life it has been like I was only half alive." After he raised over 6 million dollars, his dream became a reality. He had built Europe's first chemical free apartment complex with the potential to provide a safe haven for over 5,000 sufferers in the Switzerland area.

The photos online are absolutely breathtaking.

Knowing that people, like Mr. Shifferle, are working towards helping people who suffer with this ugly disease, is truly inspirational. He offers eight powerful words, "Today, this building symbolizes our emergence from invisibility." And I cannot help but recall that small, dilapidated motel in Deerfield Beach and wonder what might have been.

Winter will come, and I understand. Invisible doors soon close and my solitary confinement will begin. I am accustomed to the doors shutting now, no longer frightened, after all these years. Familiar, bearable, like a pair of old gloves, tattered and worn, I will sit in isolation.

When snow comes during my imprisonment, the beauty is indescribable. Garbage tossed along our country roadside, suddenly glistens as the sun shines, reflecting beauty from tiny, snow-covered heaps of junk. Only God could make such things beautiful by just his touch. Only a creator could make one pause in awe, of frozen waters, once running rampant over the rocks, in our creek.

Only an Almighty being can know the suffering and isolation we MCS sufferers feel during this beautiful time. And for this alone, we may rest in our prison, assured that spring will come, and our doors will open a little wider.

C.S. Lewis wrote, "When I became a man, I put away childish things, including the fear of childishness and the desire to be very grown up." I still love to bundle up and go outdoors, briefly, for the chance to make a snow angel, when the flakes finally fall. I can, at least, venture out to our backyard, without the prison doors, grumbling and creaking, beckoning me to quickly return before the alarm rings. And I pause, and quietly whisper, "God bless us all."

18

I do know some things. I know that part of my heart will never heal from the loss of my mother at such a tender age. Growing older, I think of her more and more, and I wonder – would she have believed me when the odds were favoring a bogus illness instead? Would she have been proud of me for my continued search for the answer? For never believing that it was not a real disease? For knowing that I was dying, just as she knew all those years ago? Am I writing this, ultimately, for her eyes?

Yes, I do know some things. For this disgusting, debilitating illness, I wear black. For my mother, I wear black. And I also wear one color of lipstick only; the one she wore, which was her favorite – red.

A few treasures, mementos small trinkets, I add from time to time to my mother's trunk, that Dad gave me so long ago, a lifetime ago, such as a Betty Crocker Homemaker of Tomorrow award I won, as a senior, when I could barely boil water; small pieces of my tattered, preemie clothes my grandmother sewed for me – patterning them after doll clothes, pieces of my children's clothes that I had smocked and sewn, a now-tarnished gold locket my grandmother/second mother left me when she died, and black and white polaroids of my parents while they were young, handsome, and in love.

One of my favorite pictures is of my parents at the baseball field behind the school they attended. Dad, thin, dressed in his scratchy, woolen, baseball uniform with glove in hand, grins from ear to ear. Although he had worked hard on the farm all day, alongside his brothers and father, he dreamed of quitting time, suiting up, and heading to the game. Playing in a K-T league meant everything to him and should anyone ask about that itchy uniform, he would simply shake his head and reply, "It doesn't bother me, just pumps me up to play." After the game, men would stuff cash into his back pocket, remnants of their winnings, from betting on his stellar performance. Everyone came to the event, supported the team, and as one could imagine, fights would occur, when words were said; fighting words, during those hot, summer nights. Why, some of the competition would hire college baseball players to pitch for them, which was against regulations, of course, and Dad's team would win anyway.

Standing close by Dad, is my beautiful mother, dressed in a short-sleeved cotton dress, fitted at the waist, with a full skirt. As my granddaughter would tell me, it definitely had twirl potential. Those timeless pumps, still popular today, adorn her feet and a simple hat sits atop her head, as she stares straight at the camera, determined and somewhat stoic. She does not smile. However, she appears healthy. And viewing this photograph, I see how lovely my mother truly was, and has remained forever young, frozen in time.

Recently, I added a comb. Not the white comb, my mother wrote of, to her sister. My comb is simple, but very costly. It is stainless, with teeth, closely fitted, allowing each strand of hair, to be pulled vigorously through its hold. Each strand will be pulled through this odd-looking comb over and over and over. It is different from any I have seen and quite different from any I have used. However, it needs to be placed in my mother's trunk. This comb relieved me of a horrible lice infestation I caught from my precious granddaughter, who caught it at school.

I would soon be in capable hands, empathetic hands, when I found a lice clinic, about an hour from our farm. Patiently, the professionals combed sections of my mid-shoulder length hair for over three and a half hours, a very labor-intensive task I knew I would be unable to attempt on my own. The manager explained this was the simplest way to get rid of the superbugs, who have become practically resistant to everything.

As a grandmother, involved with my grandchildren, the possibility to catch lice is great. She said this just proved I was a loving grandmother. I smiled, as I tried not to grab handfuls of my hair and yank.

19

After all the research, downloaded papers, and current data compilations, I find Dr. Robbins to still be correct – "No cure for this illness." Yes, I was given a life sentence, a life sentence with its own built-in prison. The doors are always open, waiting. You will never be free.

For me, in '02, frightened, confused, and so very sick, hope did appear, finally, in the form of a book. Hope will be where you least expect it, just as we have heard and read, through books, lectures, and inspirational tapes.

As we entertain angels unaware, someone or something, may give you the strength to continue forward, regardless of the adversity, the pain, and the paralyzing fear. Then, will come the joy. Then, will come the peace that passes all understanding.

Regardless of our crosses we bear, our "will," deep inside, is still strong and mighty, giving us the courage to get up each morning, dress, and look toward this new day, as the true gift we are given.

With a researcher's hands placing the next slide under their microscope, for the tenth or maybe, the hundredth experiment, they are determined to never give up knowing today might be the day for that breakthrough. And these scientists plan to succeed.

Of course, I had hoped to find even more understanding and awareness when beginning this journey, but sadly, the general population does not see us as having an actual "illness." Thankfully, I did find some measurable and objective data for the diagnosis of MCS. With this information finely honed like my grandfather's wooden instrument, dare

I believe things are changing? Are lines once drawn in the sand now blurred by the winds of enlightenment? Are eyes beginning to open? I, too, once was blind, but now I see. The simple truth is very clear – we are here and we aren't going anywhere. In fact, there is nowhere else to go.

I recall, from the beginning of time, the diseased lepers, who by law, had to shout "Leper" when they entered the village, to ensure the crowds would become aware and move at a safe distance, as they passed. This law offered a very primitive solution, in an attempt to prevent the spread of a very dreadful, very contagious, debilitating disease. Too numerous to count, I often dared to announce, "MCS sufferer," to allow people time to step aside as I quickly made my way through the crowd. The difference, however, is that I am not contagious, just dreaded.

So, for now, as Proust wrote so long ago in his book Remembrance of Things Past, against my heart, I must bid you adieu. I have a white comb to deliver.

Epilogue

Today, I am wrinkling – still the face of a rat, shriveling, and a walking, breathing miracle.

Funny thing about miracles. They are simple. They happen in the wee hours of the morning or the darkest of nights, or even in a delivery room in 1955.

Glossary

Alzheimer's disease – progressive mental deterioration that can occur in middle or old age, due to generalized degeneration of the brain. It is the most common cause of premature senility; a type of dementia that causes problems with memory, thinking, and behavior.

Antibodies – a blood protein produced in response to and counteracting a specific antigen; they combine chemically with substances which the body recognizes as alien, such as bacteria, viruses, and foreign substances in the blood.

Antigens – any substance foreign to the body that evokes an immune response either alone or after forming a complex with a larger molecule (such as a protein) and that is capable of binding with a product (such as an antibody or T cell) of the immune response.

Autoimmunity disease – a condition in which your immune system mistakenly attacks your body; normally, the immune system can tell the difference between foreign cells and your own cells. In an autoimmune disease, the immune system mistakes part of your body as foreign.

Biomarker – a biological molecule found in blood, other body fluids, or tissues that is a sign of a normal or abnormal process, or of a condition or disease. A biomarker may be used to see how well the body responds to a treatment for a disease or condition.

Blood-brain barrier – a network of blood vessels and tissue that is made up of closely spaced cells and helps keep harmful substances from reaching the brain.

Calcium – a mineral found mainly in the hard part of bones, where it is stored; is essential for healthy bones and is also important for muscle contraction, heart action, and normal blood clotting.

Central nervous system – the part of the nervous system which in vertebrates consists of the brain and spinal cord, to which sensory impulses are transmitted and from which motor impulses pass out; and which coordinates the activity of the entire nervous system.

Environmental and Occupational Health – concerned with the health effects of exposures to air and water pollution, pesticides, organic solvents, dusts and physical hazards, which occur in the environment, the home or the workplace.

Gamma globulin – a protein fraction of blood rich in antibodies.

Genetic polymorphism – a polymorphic variant of a gene can lead to abnormal expression of, or to the production of an abnormal form of the said protein; this abnormality may cause or be associated with a disease.

Glutathione – a tripeptide composed of three amino acids (cysteine, glutamic acid, and glycine) present in most tissue; acts as an antioxidant, a free radical scavenger and a detoxifying agent.

Hydrocarbon – organic compound made of two elements, carbon and hydrogen.

IgG – a class of antibodies that facilitate the phagocytic destruction of microorganisms foreign to the body, that bind and activate; and that are the only antibodies to cross the placenta from mother to fetus.

Intradermal skin tests – evaluate the person's immune system by injecting the antigens to which the patient may have been seriously sensitized (Dr. Robbins' clinic utilized these tests).

Magnesium – a mineral involved in main processes in the body including nerve signaling, the building of healthy bones, and normal muscle contraction; about 350 enzymes are known to depend on magnesium.

Mitochondria – organelles found in the cells of every complex organism, producing about 90% of the energy that cells need to survive; essentially, a sub-compartment inside our tiny cells.

Multiple chemical sensitivity – a complex chronic condition which manifests itself as a result of low-level exposures to certain everyday chemicals.

Multiple sclerosis – an immune-mediated process in which an abnormal response of the body's immune system is directed against the central nervous system; when the myelin or nerve fibers – the fatty substance that surrounds and insulates the nerve fibers, is damaged or destroyed, and the messages within the central nervous system are altered or stopped completely.

Nerve growth factor – a neurotrophic factor and neuropeptide primarily in the regulation of growth, proliferation, and survival of certain target neurons.

Neurodegenerative disease – a term for a range of conditions which primarily affect the neurons in the human brain. Neurons are the building blocks of the nervous system which includes the brain and spinal cord. Caused by the progressive death of neurons in different regions of the nervous system. The progressive loss of nerve cells is what gives rise to the neurological and neuropsychological signs and symptoms characteristic of each of these disorders.

Neuropathy – an abnormal and usually degenerative state of the nervous system or nerves.

Neuropeptides – are small, protein-like molecules used by neurons to communicate with each other, signaling molecules that influence the activity of the brain and the body in very specific ways.

Neurotoxicity – a form of toxicity in which a biological, chemical, or physical agent produces an adverse effect on the structure or function of the central and/or nervous system. Generally manifested as a continuum of symptoms and effects, which depend on the nature of the chemical, the dose, the duration of the exposure, and the traits of the exposed individual.

Nitric oxide – a colorless toxic gas formed in many reactions in which nitric acid is reduced, as in reaction with copper. It reacts immediately with oxygen to form nitrogen dioxide; in the body it controls blood flow to the tissues, acting as a blood vessel relaxant; a molecule that our body produces to help its 50 trillion cells communicate with each other by transmitting signals throughout the entire body.

Parkinson's disease – a progressive disease of the nervous system marked by tremor, muscular rigidity, and slow, imprecise movement, chiefly affecting middle-aged and elderly people. Associated with the degeneration of the basal ganglia of the brain and a deficiency of the neurotransmitter dopamine.

Patch tests – dilute solution of each allergen is placed directly on the skin and covered with gauze. In 48 to 72 hours, the appearance of redness, vesicles, itching, or swelling shows a positive reaction.

Peptides – a compound consisting of two or more amino acids linked in a chain; these simply are just small proteins. Intake and production of all the amino acids are necessary for production of all the peptides needed for the body to work efficiently. As aging occurs, stress, diet, physical changes reduce the amino acids in the body naturally.

Peripheral nervous system – the nervous system that is outside of the brain and spinal cord. PQQ – a compound to benefit the mitochondria in the body; boosts the mitochondria health.

Psychosomatic – of, relating to, concerned with, or involving both mind and body; concerned with bodily symptoms caused by mental or emotional disturbance.

Scratch test – allergens introduced to the patient's skin with a special tool or needle. Test sites are examined 30 to 40 minutes later and compared to a control site; redness, itching, or swelling shows a positive reaction.

S.O. – streptolysin O, one of a group of filterable hemolysins derived from Group A betahemolytic streptococci; a method for reducing scar tissue by administering the effective amount in a pharmaceutically acceptable vehicle – intramuscular, sublingual, intravenous,

subcutaneous, intrathecal, inhalation, and topical, administered in a dose from 0.01 units to 10 u nits; found to be effective against any scar tissue, including surgical scars, acne scars, trauma induced scars, and burn scars.

T cells – originate in the blood marrow and mature in the thymus, attack foreign or abnormal cells and regulate cell-mediated immunity.

Toxins – a poisonous substance that is a specific product of the metabolic activities of a living organism and is usually very unstable, notably toxic when introduced into the tissues, and typically capable of inducing antibody formation.

Vitamin C buffered powder – an antioxidant, with buffering minerals magnesium m, potassium m, and calcium m to allow higher doses for supporting proper muscle relaxation and contraction.

Addendum

2015 Brussels International Scientific Declaration on Electromagnetic Hypersensitivity and Multiple Chemical Sensitivity.

Following the 5th Paris Appeal Congress that took place on the 13 May 2015 at the Royal Academy of Medicine, Brussels, Belgium.

Recalling the pioneering work of the American allergologist Theron

G. Randolph to whom we owe the first clinical description in 1962 of what is today commonly called multiple chemical sensitivity.

Recalling the scientific workshop on multiple chemical sensitivity which was conducted in 1992 at the request of the U.S. Environmental Protection Agency.

Recalling the WHO technical report "Environmental Health Criteria 137: Electromagnetic Fields (300Hz to 300GHz)," published under the joint sponsorship of the United Nations Environment Program, the International Radiation Protection Association and the World Health Organization, 1993, Geneva.

Recalling the report of the international workshop on multiple chemical sensitivity which took place on 21–23 February 1996 in Berlin, Germany.

Recalling the United Nations Economic Commission for Europe (UNECE) Convention on Access to Information, Public Participation in Decision-Making and Access to Justice in Environmental Matters, adopted on 25 June 1998 in Aarhus, Denmark.

Recalling the COST 244 international workshop on Electromagnetic Fields and Non-specific Health Symptoms, 19–20 September 1998, Graz, Austria.

Recalling the 1999 Consensus on Multiple Chemical Sensitivity adopted following the National Institute of Health 1999 Atlanta Conference on the Health Impact of Chemical Exposures during the Gulf War, United States.

Recalling the Paris Appeal international declaration on diseases caused by chemical pollution which was proclaimed on 7 May 2004 at UNESCO Paris headquarters.

Recalling the WHO Workshop on Sensitivity of Children to EMF Exposure, Istanbul, Turkey, 9–10 June 2004.

Recalling the WHO Workshop on guiding public health policy in areas of scientific uncertainty, Ottawa, Canada. 11–13 July 2005.

Recalling the WHO Fact sheet N.296, December 2005 "Electromagnetic fields and public health: Electromagnetic hypersensitivity."

Recalling the report of Margaret E. Sears entitled "The Medical Perspective on Environmental Sensitivities," which was prepared for the Canadian Human Rights Commission and published in May 2007.

Recalling the 2007/2012/2014 Bio initiative Report: A Rationale for Biologically-based Public Exposure Standards for Electromagnetic Fields (ELF and RF).

Recalling the European Parliament resolution of 2 April 2009 on health concerns associated with electromagnetic fields."

Recalling the "Scientific Panel on Electromagnetic Field Health Risks: Consensus Points, Recommendations, and Rationales," held at Seletun, Norway, 17–21 November 2009.

Recalling the 13 May 2011 meeting gathering NGOs at the WHO headquarters (Geneva) asking for the recognition of MCS and EHS as environmental diseases and their inclusion in the International Classification of Diseases ICD-10.

Recalling the virtual platform created by WHO, following this meeting, in order to get an ICD code for MCS and EHS.

Recalling the Resolution N.1815 of the Parliamentary Assembly, Council of Europe, adopted 27 May 2011. "The potential dangers of electromagnetic fields and their effect on the environment."

Recalling the Progress Report June 2013–2014 of the International EMF Project launched by WHO in 1996.

Recalling the WHO Fact sheet N.193, October 2014 "Electromagnetic fields and public health: mobile phones."

Recalling the recent International EMF Scientist Appeal to the U.N. to protect Humans and Wildlife from Electromagnetic Fields and Wireless Technology, 11 May 2015.

Considering that the chemical and electromagnetic environment is deteriorating globally, and that so-called electromagnetic hypersensitivity (EHS) and multiple chemical sensitivity (MCS) are an escalating worldwide health problem, affecting industrialized as well as developing countries – we, physicians, acting in accordance with the Hippocratic Oath – we, scientists, acting in the name of the scientific truth – we all, medical doctors and researchers working in different countries worldwide, hereby state in full dependence of judgment:

*that a high and growing number of persons are suffering from EHS and MCS worldwide and that EHS and MCS affect women, men, and children;

*that on the basis of the presently available peer-reviewed scientific evidence of adverse health effects of electromagnetic fields (EMFs) and various chemicals, and on the basis of clinical and biological investigations of patients, EHS is associated with exposure to EMFs and MCS with chemical exposure;

*that many frequencies of the electromagnetic spectrum (radio and microwave-frequencies as well as low and extremely low frequencies) and multiple chemicals are involved in the occurrence of EHS and MCS respectively;

*that the trigger for illness can be acute high intensity exposure or chronic very low intensity exposure and that reversibility can be obtained with a natural environment characterized by limited levels of anthropogenic EMFs and chemicals;

*that current case-control epidemiological studies and provocative studies aiming at reproducing EHS and/or MCS are scientifically difficult to construct and due to the present design flaws are in fact not suitable to prove or disprove causality; in particular because objective inclusion/exclusion criteria and endpoint evaluation criteria need to be more clearly defined; because responses to EMFs/chemicals are highly individual and depend on a variety of exposure parameters; and finally because test conditions are often reducing signal-to-noise ratio thereby obscuring evidence of a possible effect;

*that the nocebo effect is not a relevant nor a valid explanation when considering scientifically valuable blind provocation studies, since objective biological markers are detectable in patients as well as animals;

*that new approaches are emerging for clinical and biological diagnosis and for monitoring of EHS and MCS including the use of reliable biomarkers;

*that EHS and MCS may be two faces of the same hypersensitivity-associated pathological condition and that this condition is causing serious consequences to health, professional, and family life;

*finally, that EHS and MCS ought therefore to be fully recognized by international and national institutions with responsibility for human health.

In view of our present scientific knowledge, we thereby stress all national and international bodies and institutions, more particularly the World Health Organization (WHO), to recognize EHS and MCS as true medical conditions which acting as sentinel diseases may create a major public health concern in years to come worldwide i.e. in all the countries implementing unrestricted use of electromagnetic field-based wireless technologies and marketed chemical substances.

Inaction is a cost to society and is not an option any more.

Although our scientific knowledge still remains to be completed, we unanimously acknowledge this serious hazard to public health, urgently requiring the recognition of this condition at all international levels, so that persons can benefit from adapted diagnostic tools and innovative treatments, and above all, major primary prevention measures are adopted and prioritized, to face this worldwide pan-epidemic in perspective.

According to the present scientific knowledge and taking into account the precautionary principle, we unanimously recommend that true information in the use of chemicals and wireless technologies be made accessible to the public and precautionary regulation measures applying particularly to children and other vulnerable population subgroups be urgently taken as it should be the case regarding chemicals in the application of the European Registration Evaluation Authorization and Restriction of Chemicals (REACH) regulation.